TREES: SENTINELS OF THE LAND

These are the trees which never give in, never give up, and inspire us by their presence.

TREES

SENTINELS OF THE LAND

DANIEL WIENER

Acacia *Bibiani, Western Region, Ghana*

Flowering Dogwood
Kingston, New York, U.S.A.

Jeffrey Pine
Mount Rose, Nevada, U.S.A.

Larch *Roundstone, County Galway, Ireland*

Sugar Maple *Montpelier, Vermont, U.S.A.*

Eucalyptus *Lowther, New South Wales, Australia*

Lodgepole Pine *Chilco Lake, British Columbia, Canada*

Elm *framed by* **Maples**   *Montreal, Quebec, Canada*

Blue Spruce *Montreal, Quebec, Canada*

Sitka Spruce
Juneau, Alaska, U.S.A.

left to right
White Spruce, Sugar Maple
Mont Tremblant,
Quebec, Canada

Trembling Aspen *Silverton, Colorado, U.S.A.*

Purple Smoke Tree
Montreal, Quebec, Canada

Rubber Trees
Krabi, Krabi Province,
Thailand

left to right
**Red Spruce, Red Maple,
Grey Birch**
Granville, Vermont, U.S.A.

Green Ash
Julesburg, Colorado, U.S.A.

Red Maple *Lac Nantel, Quebec, Canada*

White Elm *Saskatoon, Saskatchewan, Canada*

Taiping, Perak, Malaysia

Ponderosa Pine *Kettle Falls, Washington, U.S.A.*

Silver Maple *Montreal, Quebec, Canada*

Red Maple *Kingston Mills, Ontario, Canada*

Radiata Pine
Beech Forest, Victoria,
Australia

Coconut Palm *Davao, Mindinao, Philippines*

Eucalyptus *Strahan, Tasmania, Australia*

Trembling Aspen *Jasper, Alberta, Canada*

Krabi, Krabi Province,
Thailand

Prescott, Arizona, U.S.A.

Lodgepole Pine *Burmis, Alberta, Canada*

Mesquite
Death Valley National Park,
California, U.S.A.

Eucalyptus *Bothwell, Tasmania, Australia*

left to right
Eastern Hemlock, White Pine *Bala, Ontario, Canada*

Silver Maple
Esopus, New York, U.S.A.

top left to center
Redbud, Cherry Blossom
Cambridge, Massachusetts,
U.S.A.

Western Hemlock
and **Red Alder**
Whistler, British Columbia,
Canada

Yew *Lac Nantel, Quebec, Canada*

Grey Birch
Longueuil, Quebec, Canada

Paper Birch
Huntsville, Ontario, Canada

Western Hemlock *Douglas, Alaska, U.S.A.*

Eucalyptus
Newman, West Australia,
Australia

European Yew
Montreal, Quebec, Canada

Oak
Columbus, Texas, U.S.A.

Western Hemlock,
Red Cedar *logs*
Gold River, British Columbia,
Canada

Ponderosa Pine *and* **Douglas Fir** *Republic, Washington, U.S.A.*

Poplar
Montreal, Quebec, Canada

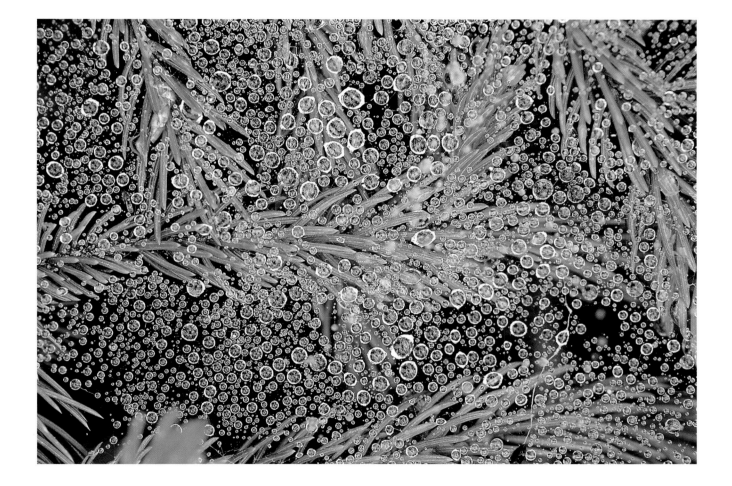

White Spruce *Lac Nantel, Quebec, Canada*

Paper Birch *Keene Valley, New York, U.S.A.*

Eucalyptus
Denmark, West Australia,
Australia

Ponderosa Pine
Running Springs,
California, U.S.A.

Credits

*Sincere thanks are extended
to Professor Jim Fyles, Department
of Natural Resource Sciences, McGill
University, and Professor Luc Brouillet,
Department of Biological Sciences,
University of Montreal. Both spent long
hours identifying the trees. In many
instances, genus and species are named.
When identification proved uncertain,
genus alone is indicated. In some photos,
identification is not possible.*

Design
*Ronan Kearney
Signa Design Communications Inc.
Montreal, QC*

Scanning, Film & Imposition
Tri-Graphiques, Montreal, QC

Printing
Friesens, Altona, MB

Distribution & Mail Order
*Priorities Plus
832 Gold Court
Battle Mountain, NV 89820
toll-free: 1-888-635-9490
fax: 702-635-9492
e-mail: prioritiesplus@the-onramp.net
web site: www.prioritiesplus.com*

ISBN Number 1-55056-581-8

Printed in Canada